SYLVIA MENDEZ

Education Equality Activist

J.M. Klein

Cavendish
Square

New York

Published in 2020 by Cavendish Square Publishing, LLC
243 5th Avenue, Suite 136, New York, NY 10016

Website: cavendishsq.com

This publication represents the opinions and views of the author based on his or her personal experience, knowledge, and research. The information in this book serves as a general guide only. The author and publisher have used their best efforts in preparing this book and disclaim liability rising directly or indirectly from the use and application of this book.

All websites were available and accurate when this book was sent to press.

Library of Congress Cataloging-in-Publication Data

Names: Klein, J. M., author.
Title: Sylvia Mendez : education equality activist / J.M. Klein.
Description: First edition. | New York : Cavendish Square, 2020. |
Series: Barrier breaker bios | Includes index. | Audience: Grade 1 to 4.
Identifiers: LCCN 2019017958 (print) | LCCN 2019022117 (ebook) | ISBN
9781502649744 (library bound) | ISBN 9781502649720 (pbk.) |
ISBN 9781502649737 (6 pack)
Subjects: LCSH: Mendez, Sylvia, 1936---Juvenile literature. | School
integration--United States--Juvenile literature. | Hispanic
Americans--Education--Juvenile literature. | Puerto Rican
women--California--Biography--Juvenile literature.
Classification: LCC LC214.2 .K6 2020 (print) | LCC LC214.2 (ebook) | DDC 379.2/63--dc23
LC record available at https://lccn.loc.gov/2019017958
LC ebook record available at https://lccn.loc.gov/2019022117

Editor: Alexis David
Copy Editor: Nathan Heidelberger
Associate Art Director: Alan Sliwinski
Designer: Christina Shults
Production Coordinator: Karol Szymczuk
Photo Research: J8 Media

The photographs in this book are used by permission and through the courtesy of:
Cover Brooks Kraft LLC/Corbis/Getty Images; p. 1 and throughout jorgen mcleman/Shutterstock.com; p. 3 and throughout Vecteezy.com; pp. 4, 24 Alex Wong/Getty Images; pp. 6, 14 Ana Venegas/The Orange County Register/ZUMAPRESS.com; p. 10 Image courtesy of the Frank Mt. Pleasant Library of Special Collections & Archives, Leatherby Libraries at Chapman University; p. 12 ClassicStock/Alamy Stock Photo; p. 15 MikeJiroch/Wikimedia Commons/File:U.S. Court House and Post Office, 312 N. Spring St. Downtown Los Angeles 20.jpg/CC BY SA 3.0;
p. 16 Courtesy http://www.Mexican-American.org; p. 17 Cindy Yamanaka/The Orange County Register/ZUMA Press; p. 19 Office of Senator Kamala Harris and US Department of Agriculture/Wikimedia Commons/File:Sylvia Mendez DYhqZKOXkAYFrkJ.jpg/PD; pp. 20, 26 Bettmann/Getty Images; pp. 22, 27 Nature and Science/Alamy Stock Photo.

Printed in the United States of America

TABLE OF CONTENTS

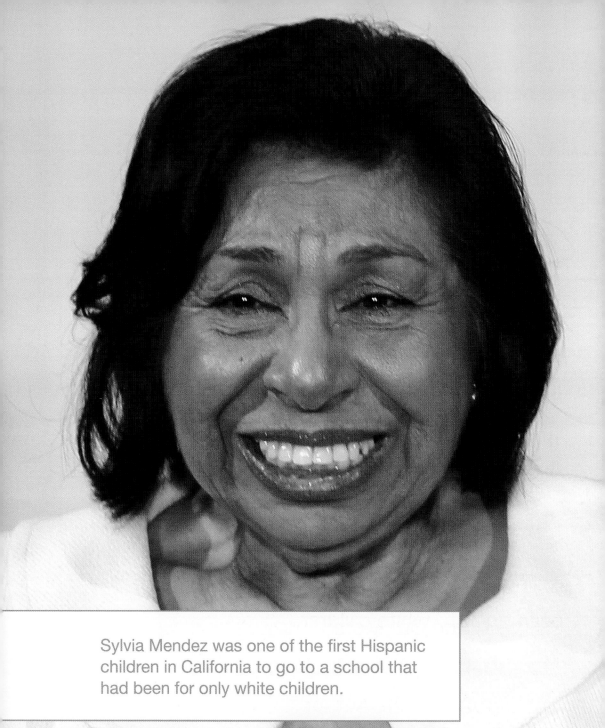

Sylvia Mendez was one of the first Hispanic children in California to go to a school that had been for only white children.

CHAPTER 1

A NEW SCHOOL FOR SYLVIA

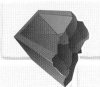

Schools today are filled with kids who have all different skin colors, but it wasn't always this way. Children used to be separated in schools. White children went to one school. Children with skin colors other than white went to other schools.

That changed—starting with Sylvia Mendez. Mendez and her brothers were the first **Hispanic** children in California to go to a school that had only been open to white children.

Now Mendez is an **activist**. An activist works to make change happen. Mendez helps other students. She works to make schools better.

A BIG MOVE

It was the early 1940s. Sylvia Mendez was eight years old. Her family had just moved to live on a farm.

The family would have more space on the farm. Their old home was in a city. It was crowded. Lots of people lived there.

Sylvia Mendez holds a book written about her childhood on the farm.

FAST FACT

Sylvia's brothers were named Gonzalo Jr. and Jerome.

GONZALO MENDEZ

Sylvia Mendez's father worked hard to help his family. Gonzalo Mendez was born in Mexico. By the 1940s, he was an American **citizen**. A citizen is a member of a country. He used to be a field worker. For years, he picked grapes and oranges. Then the family moved to Westminster, California. Gonzalo rented his own farm. Gonzalo was now the boss. He became a businessman. He learned how to get people to work together. This helped him fight for Sylvia and her brothers.

The new farm was in Westminster, California. It was on 40 acres (16 hectares) of land.

TWO SCHOOLS

There were two schools around the Mendez family farm. Hoover Elementary School was small and didn't look very nice. It didn't have a playground for the students to use.

The 17th Street School was close to Mendez's house. It looked nice. Tall trees grew outside. The lawn was green and pretty. The school had lots of books. It also had a playground.

Mendez loved the playground. She wanted to climb the monkey bars.

SAD NEWS FOR SYLVIA

However, the 17th Street School said Mendez couldn't go there. Her brothers couldn't go either. Mendez was Hispanic. She had dark skin. She had a Mexican last name. Her father was from Mexico. Her mother was from Puerto Rico.

Only children with white skin could go to the nice school. Children who looked like Sylvia Mendez went to Hoover Elementary School. This is called **segregation**.

THE FIGHT BEGINS

Mendez's father didn't think this was right. His name was Gonzalo Mendez. Gonzalo wanted Sylvia and her brothers to be able to go to the good school. It had better books. They would learn more there.

Gonzalo decided he would fight. He would find a way for his children to go to the good school.

FAST FACT

Mendez adopted two girls when she grew up.

A class photo from the 17th Street School shows Sylvia's brother Gonzalo Jr. in the front row (*fourth from the left*).

CHAPTER 2

THE COURT BATTLE

The school Mendez had to go to wasn't nice. It only had two rooms. The books were old. It didn't have a playground. The students had to eat outside. Outside there were no trees—only cows. The cows smelled bad.

Mendez walked by the nice school every day. She felt sad. She still wanted to climb the monkey bars.

SYLVIA'S PARENTS WORK HARD

Mendez's father worked to get her into the 17th Street School. Mendez watched her father leave every morning. He would be gone all day. Mendez's mother took care of the farm instead.

Gonzalo Mendez talked to lots of people. He talked to the school principal. He talked to the **school board**. He talked to community leaders.

Sylvia wanted to play on the monkey bars at the nicer school.

He talked to other mothers and fathers. However, he couldn't get his children into the good school.

Then someone gave Gonzalo an idea. Gonzalo could take the school board to **court**, and a **judge** would decide. Gonzalo also got help. Four other Mexican American fathers joined him. They would all go to court.

SYLVIA PREPARES

Sylvia Mendez got ready for court every morning. School officials had said Hispanic students were dirty. They said students like Mendez had lice. They said they couldn't speak English.

FAST FACT

Mendez's court case grew to represent five thousand Hispanic children in California.

Mendez's parents are photographed here.

Mendez knew this was wrong. She wasn't dirty. She tried to look her best every day. She practiced how she would answer questions.

One of the other Hispanic students answered questions in court. She spoke in perfect English. That showed that school officials were wrong. Hispanic students did understand English.

THE DECISION

In 1946, the judge decided the case. He said the 17th Street School was wrong. Children could not be separated by skin color. A school had to be open to all children. It didn't matter what their skin color was or if they were rich or poor.

Mendez was so excited, and so were her parents.

Then the school board tried again to keep students separated. They went to a bigger court. They asked other judges to decide. Mendez and her family had to go back to court.

Here is where the Mendez case was first heard.

This time, the court was farther away. It was in San Francisco, California.

In 1947, the second court decided. It said the Mendez family was right. Sylvia and her brothers could go to the 17th Street School.

Los Angeles Times
February 19, 1946

RULING GIVES MEXICAN CHILDREN EQUAL RIGHTS

Segregation of Mexican school-children from others in four Santa Ana school districts yesterday was held by U.S. Judge Paul J. McCormick to be a violation of their guarantees of equal rights under the 14th Amendment of the Constitution.

The opinion was written in connection with a suit filed by five parents of Mexican children asking for relief and an injunction forbidding the school district trustees from placing the Mexican children in separate schools.

The school districts involved were Westminster, Orange Grove, Santa Ana City Schools and El Modeno. The suit also named the superintendents and trustees of the districts.

Judge McCormick overruled a defense contention that segregation being an educational matter, it fell under the jurisdiction of the State. He held that inasmuch as violations of the 14th Amendment were indicated, the Federal court had a right to intervene.

"The evidence clearly shows," the opinion states, "that Spanish-speaking children are retarded in learning English by lack of exposure to its use because of segregation . . .

"It is also established by the record that the methods of segregation prevalent in the defendant school districts foster antagonisms in the children and suggest inferiority among them where none exists."

Judge McCormick at the same time ordered Attorney David C. Marcus, who represented the parents in the action, to file a petition for an injunction against the defendants within 10 days, indicating that the restraining order would be approved upon the findings of his opinion.

The *Los Angeles Times* announces the *Mendez v. Westminster* case results.

A BAD FIRST DAY OF SCHOOL

Mendez was now eleven years old. Finally she could go to the 17th Street School. Her first day was hard. Other students called her names. They said she shouldn't be there. They told her to go back to the other school. They said she didn't belong.

FAST FACT

In California, two schools are named after Mendez's parents, and one elementary school is named for Mendez herself.

Sylvia Mendez points at herself as a child in a painting.

Mendez cried. She came home from school. She told her mother she didn't want to go back.

Mendez's mother listened. "This is why we fought," she said. They fought to show that Mendez belonged at a good school. Mendez understood. She had

MENDEZ GROWS UP

When Mendez grew up, she became a nurse. She was a nurse for thirty-three years. She took care of lots of people. She became an assistant director at a big hospital.

Then her mother got sick. Mendez retired. She took care of her mother instead.

Mendez's mother told her she needed to tell her story. At first, Mendez said she couldn't. She said she was only a nurse. She wasn't an activist.

However, her mother told her someone had to speak up, so Mendez sent letters to schools. She also went to court again. She changed what schools taught. Now all students in California learn about Sylvia Mendez.

Sylvia Mendez

ONE OF THE FIRST STUDENTS OF MEXICAN DESCENT TO ATTEND AN ALL-WHITE SCHOOL IN CALIFORNIA

Mendez is now an activist who works to help students.

thought the fight was about the playground, but now she knew it was about more. Her parents had fought for her future.

She went back to school. She held her head up. She didn't listen to the mean voices. She did make friends—with children of all different skin colors.

In 1954, seven years after the Mendez case, another court case ended segregation in schools across the country.

CHAPTER 3

SCHOOLS TODAY

Thanks to the Mendez family, schools in California changed. Schools couldn't only be for white children. Hispanic children could go to nearby schools, just like Sylvia Mendez. They could play on the playgrounds. White students and Hispanic students were in the same classroom.

MORE CHANGES

One year later, California schools changed for students of other races. A judge said Asian American students couldn't be turned away from schools—neither could Native Americans.

Change also happened outside of schools. Public swimming pools and parks used to be only for white people. Hispanic people could only swim at certain times. That started slowly changing after the Mendez case.

Sylvia Mendez now speaks to children and adults, telling them about her parents' fight to help Hispanic children.

STILL SEPARATE

However, the rest of America was still separate. In other states, white children went to one school, and black children went to a different school.

Seven years later, this changed too. In 1954, another court case was decided. This case was named after another girl. Her name was Linda Brown. Linda Brown was black. She wasn't allowed to go to a white school. Her parents fought for her, just like Mendez's parents had.

This court case ended segregation across America. Today, students of all races and backgrounds can go

FAST FACT

Sylvia Mendez received the Presidential Medal of Freedom in 2011.

President Obama awards Mendez the Presidential Medal of Freedom.

to school together. Mendez's court case helped start the movement toward equality.

SYLVIA MENDEZ TODAY

Today, Sylvia Mendez visits schools across the country. She talks to students. She tells them about how important school is. She tells them about her parents' work.

Mendez also warns about a new problem in schools. She says money now separates children. Rich neighborhoods have better schools. They have better books. They have better

THURGOOD MARSHALL

Many people helped the Mendez family. One of them was Thurgood Marshall.

Marshall was a lawyer. He helped during the second court case. He wrote letters to the court. He explained why Sylvia Mendez should haven been able to go to the white school. He came up with legal reasons.

A few years later, Marshall used those same reasons again. He was the lawyer for Linda Brown. Marshall explained why Linda Brown should be able to go to a white school too. He won. That court case ended segregation everywhere.

Thurgood Marshall later became the first black judge on the Supreme Court. The Supreme Court is the most important court in the United States.

Thurgood Marshall helped during the Mendez court case.
He later worked to end segregation across the country.

teachers. Schools in poor neighborhoods aren't as
good. Sometimes poor schools only have students
of one race.

Mendez says this is a new kind of segregation.
She's speaking up about the problem. She works

to make change happen. Mendez teaches about segregation. She tells students to work hard. She wants them to go to class. She wants everyone to get a good education. She says that's why her parents worked so hard. Her parents fought so all students could get a good education.

Here is the stamp that honors Mendez's court case.

FAST FACT

In 2007, the US Postal Service made a stamp in honor of the Mendez court case.

TIMELINE

1936 Sylvia Mendez is born.

1945 Gonzalo Mendez and four other Mexican American fathers file a lawsuit against the Westminster school board.

1946 A judge rules that all children should be allowed to go to school together in *Mendez v. Westminster*.

1947 A court of appeals upholds *Mendez v. Westminster*.

1948 Sylvia Mendez and her brothers are finally allowed to attend the 17th Street School.

1954 Segregation becomes illegal everywhere because of *Brown v. Board of Education of Topeka*.

2011 Mendez receives the Presidential Medal of Freedom.

GLOSSARY

activist A person who works to make change happen.

citizen A person who is a member of a country and has specific rights.

court A place where legal decisions are made.

Hispanic A person who is from (or whose parents or grandparents are from) a country where Spanish is the primary language.

judge A person who decides what is right and what is wrong in a court case.

school board A group of people in charge of making decisions for local schools.

segregation The act of keeping two groups apart for racial, religious, or other reasons.

FIND OUT MORE

BOOKS

Tonatiuh, Duncan. *Separate Is Never Equal: Sylvia Mendez and Her Family's Fight for Desegregation.* New York, NY: Abrams Books for Young Readers, 2014.

Wolny, Philip. *Sylvia Mendez: Civil Rights Activist.* New York, NY: Rosen Central, 2018.

WEBSITE

Sylvia Mendez's Website

http://sylviamendezinthemendezvswestminster.com

VIDEO

Mendez v. Westminster

https://bit.ly/2IgVOrZ

INDEX

ABOUT THE AUTHOR

J.M. Klein used to work in California as a journalist. While a reporter, she covered education and schools. She's the author of the hi-lo series for struggling readers *The Totally Secret Diary of Dani D.*